WISH, A MUSICAL

A full-length musical by
Paul Lewis

Based on the novel *Wish* by Barbara O'Connor

www.youthplays.com
info@youthplays.com
424-703-5315

COPYRIGHT RULES TO REMEMBER

1. To produce this play, you must receive prior written permission from YouthPLAYS and pay the required royalty.

2. You must pay a royalty each time the play is performed in the presence of audience members outside of the cast and crew. Royalties are due whether or not admission is charged, whether or not the play is presented for profit, for charity or for educational purposes, or whether or not anyone associated with the production is being paid.

3. No changes, including cuts or additions, are permitted to the script without written prior permission from YouthPLAYS.

4. Do not copy this book or any part of it without written permission from YouthPLAYS.

5. Credit to the author and YouthPLAYS is required on all programs and other promotional items associated with this play's performance.

When you pay royalties, you are recognizing the hard work that went into creating the play and making a statement that a play is something of value. We think this is important, and we hope that everyone will do the right thing, thus allowing playwrights to generate income and continue to create wonderful new works for the stage.

Plays are owned by the playwrights who wrote them. Violating a playwright's copyright is a very serious matter and violates both United States and international copyright law. Infringement is punishable by actual damages and attorneys' fees, statutory damages of up to $150,000 per incident, and even possible criminal sanctions. **Infringement is theft. Don't do it.**

Have a question about copyright? Please contact us by email at info@youthplays.com or by phone at 424-703-5315. When in doubt, please ask.

CAST OF CHARACTERS

CHARLIE, a girl of 11.

BERTHA, Charlie's aunt, early 40s or older.

GUS, Charlie's uncle, early 40s or older.

JACKIE, Charlie's 18-year-old sister.

HOWARD, a boy of 11 or 12.

BURL, Howard's brother, around 19.

LANIE, Howard's sister, around 16.

AUDREY, a Sunday school classmate, around 14.

WISHBONE, a dog, portrayed by a live dog, puppet or costumed performer.

ENSEMBLE, speaking roles include SOCIAL WORKER, BUS DRIVER, TEACHER, BETTY (a beautician).

Additional ensemble members may be added to several of the songs (1, 4, 10, 11) or as otherwise desired by your production to accommodate 13-25+ performers for school, youth or community theatre productions.

The show may be performed by a cast as small as 8 with the following doubling plan:

Jackie doubles as Audrey and Ensemble; Social Worker doubles as Teacher, Betty and Ensemble; Gus doubles as Bus Driver and Burl.

SETTING

In the recent past, mostly in and around Colby, a fictional town in the Blue Ridge Mountains of western North Carolina. The settings may be simply suggestive.

SONGS

Sweet Mountain Bluebird	Charlie, Ensemble
Shelves Full of Mason Jars	Bertha
One Fine Day	Charlie
Bible Bucks	Lanie, Burl, Howard, Audrey, Sunday School Teacher
With a Dog Like You	Charlie
Wish	Charlie, Howard
Carolina Angel, Jacqueline	Burl, Lanie
Nothing's Gonna Change	Jackie
Let's Draw a Map	Howard
Where You Gone To, Wishbone?	Lanie, Burl, Audrey, Betty, Gus, Ensemble
Finale: Going Home	Lanie, Howard, Charlie, Ensemble

QR CODE FOR SCORE

PRODUCTION NOTES

A number of the songs are bluegrass pieces (1, 4, 7, 10, 11). Bluegrass invites togetherness and improvisation. Having several of the performers play guitar, banjo or other instruments would add an authentic dimension to any staging of this musical.

DEDICATION

Special thanks to Mary Guaraldi for her many invaluable insights, which helped shape the development of this script.

SCENE 1

(CHARLIE stands alone onstage, looking out, holding a diary. Nearby, in darkness, is the SOCIAL WORKER.)

SOCIAL WORKER: Charlemagne. Did you hear what I just said?

CHARLIE: Yes.

SOCIAL WORKER: Do you have any questions?

CHARLIE: Who are you again, exactly?

(Lights up on the Social Worker.)

SOCIAL WORKER: I'm Miss Reynolds. A social worker—a child placement specialist.

CHARLIE: And how long are you going to be "placing" me with these hillbilly people?

SOCIAL WORKER: They're not some hillbilly people, honey. They're your Aunt Bertha and Uncle Gus. They're kin. Family.

CHARLIE: I've never even met them before. And you didn't answer my question.

SOCIAL WORKER: Honey, your mama stays in bed all day with the curtains drawn and empty soda cans everywhere. By all appearances, she hasn't cooked a proper meal for you and Jacqueline in months. Your father, Richard—

CHARLIE: Scrappy.

(Beat.)

SOCIAL WORKER: Scrappy.

CHARLIE: That's what everyone calls him, because he's always getting into fights.

SOCIAL WORKER: Well, your father...Scrappy...is in jail. Again.

CHARLIE: Yes, I know all that. But you still haven't answered my question. How long do I have to stay with these so-called kin of mine?

SOCIAL WORKER: Just until your mama has her feet back on the ground, honey. Try it out for the summer. If you're unhappy in Colby, you just get in touch or have your Aunt Bertha get in touch, and I'll try to find you a placement closer to Raleigh. *(Handing Charlie her card:)* Here.

CHARLIE: What's this?

SOCIAL WORKER: My card. With my phone number.

CHARLIE: What if I lose that card? You'd better write it all down here, in my diary.

(Music begins.)

1. Sweet Mountain Bluebird

(Charlie faces the audience to sing:)

THE GROWN-UPS HAVE DECIDED NOW.
THEY'VE HAD THEIR FINAL SAY.
MAMA'S LOST CONTROL
AND SO THEY'RE SENDING ME AWAY.
THERE'S A BUS THAT LEAVES TOMORROW
AT FIVE MINUTES AFTER TEN.
THEY SAY TO PACK A BAG. WHAT THEN?
MAMA, OH, WHY CAN'T YOU
PUT YOUR FEET UPON THE GROUND?
I DO IT EVERY DAY
AND AS YOU SEE, I'M STILL AROUND

(Charlie looks at her feet planted firmly on the ground.)

How hard is that, honestly?

HOW COME THEY PLACED MY SISTER
IN A FAMILY WITH A POOL

AND SHIP ME OFF TO RELATIVES
AND AN UNFAMILIAR SCHOOL?

(Music continues. Lights up on the Social Worker, who hands Charlie's diary back to her.)

Well? How come?

SOCIAL WORKER: Charlemagne: as you know, Jackie is best friends with Carol Lee, and they both just graduated from high school. Carol Lee's parents agreed to take her in, but they simply can't accommodate both of you.

CHARLIE: Can you please stop calling me Charlemagne? My name is Charlie.

(Music continues, taking on a bluegrass vibe. The Social Worker exits. The BUS DRIVER enters. A suitcase appears by Charlie's side.)

BUS DRIVER: Now boarding the Carolina Local, with stops in Greensboro, Kernersville, Winston-Salem, Lenoir, Boone, Linville, Marion and Asheville.

(Music continues. ENSEMBLE enters as travelers, each with a suitcase. Handing tickets to the Bus Driver, each takes their place inside a space representing the inside of a bus. Charlie is the last one in line.)

Hello, young lady.

CHARLIE: They told me at the ticket window that this is the bus to Colby.

BUS DRIVER: Yes, it is.

CHARLIE: But you didn't announce it.

BUS DRIVER: Oh, don't you worry. I'll let you off there. Colby's between Linville Falls and Marion, but it's such a tiny little speck of a place that I don't even bother to announce it.

CHARLIE: *(To audience:)* Oh, great. This is getting better all the time.

> *(Music continues and builds. The sounds of a bus engine. An animated map shows a bus progressing from Raleigh into western North Carolina as the hands of a clock spin forward.)*

WE'VE BEEN SWITCHBACKING THROUGH MOUNTAINS
SINCE TEN MINUTES AFTER FOUR.
IT'S VERY CLEAR TO ME
WE'RE NOT IN RALEIGH ANYMORE.
HOUSES ON THE HILLSIDES
'BOUT TO TUMBLE DOWN AND FALL.
FRONT PORCHES, YELLOW DOGS AND ALL.
MAMA, OH, WHY CAN'T YOU
PUT YOUR FEET UPON THE GROUND?
I DO IT EVERY DAY
AND AS YOU SEE, I'M STILL AROUND.

> *(Music continues.)*

Excuse me, Mr. Bus Driver. How much further until we get to Colby?

BUS DRIVER: Colby's up the road just another twenty miles or so. I take it that someone's going to be meeting you there.

CHARLIE: Relatives, I guess—if they happen to remember. I'm only going to be there 'til my mama remembers to get out of bed in the morning, you see. So don't be too surprised if you see me back on this bus in a few days, heading back to Raleigh... Oh! Wait a minute! What's *that*?

BUS DRIVER: That's an Eastern bluebird. 'Though they call it a mountain bluebird around here.

CHARLIE: Thank you! *(Addressing the audience directly:)* If you see and identify a new bird—one you've never seen before—you get to make a wish. So I better go ahead and do that *now.*

(Charlie closes her eyes momentarily, then opens them again for another glimpse of the bird.)

IT'S A STRANGE AND LONESOME ROAD
THIS OL' STATE ROUTE TWO-TWENTY-ONE
SO MY HEART SKIPPED LIKE A TOAD
WHEN I SAW YOU IN THE SUN.
SWEET MOUNTAIN BLUEBIRD
FLYING TOWARD TOMORROW
WITHOUT A CARE OR SORROW,
SAILING HIGH ABOVE THE TREES.
SWEET MOUNTAIN BLUEBIRD
WON'T YOU TAKE ME TO THE SKY WITH YOU
TEACH ME HOW TO FLY WITH YOU
OH, MOUNTAIN BLUEBIRD, PLEASE?

ENSEMBLE: IT'S A SLOW AND CURVY ROAD
THAT WINDS THROUGH HICKORY AND PINE
PAST TOWNS THAT LOOK LIKE
POSTCARDS FROM A VERY DIFFERENT TIME
BUT NO MATTER WHERE I TRAVEL
AND NO MATTER WHERE I ROAM,
WHEN I SEE YOU SAILING O'ER THE HILLS,
THEN I KNOW THAT I'M ALMOST HOME
SWEET MOUNTAIN BLUEBIRD
FLYING TOWARD TOMORROW
WITHOUT A CARE OR SORROW,
SAILING HIGH ABOVE THE TREES.
SWEET MOUNTAIN BLUEBIRD
WON'T YOU TAKE ME TO THE SKY WITH YOU
TEACH ME HOW TO FLY WITH YOU
OH, MOUNTAIN BLUEBIRD, PLEASE?

CHARLIE AND ENSEMBLE: SWEET MOUNTAIN
BLUEBIRD
FLYING TOWARD TOMORROW
WITHOUT A CARE OR SORROW,
SAILING HIGH AND FEELING FREE.
SWEET MOUNTAIN BLUEBIRD
WON'T YOU TAKE ME TO THE SKY WITH YOU
TEACH ME HOW TO FLY WITH YOU
OH, MOUNTAIN BLUEBIRD, PLEASE?
PLEASE, MOUNTAIN BLUEBIRD, PLEASE!

(Song ends. All exit except Charlie, alone onstage with her suitcase. The sound of a bus pulling away. We are now on the outskirts of Colby.)

BERTHA: *(Off:)* Charlemagne? Charlemagne? Is that you?

(BERTHA enters.)

CHARLIE: My name's Charlie. Who are you?

BERTHA: Why, I'm your Aunt Bertha—your mom's sister. But you can call me plain old Bertha. Now, family or not, I don't take much to hugging folks I've never met, so how about a good old-fashioned handshake?

CHARLIE: Okay, I guess.

BERTHA: Pleased to meet you, Charlie. Gus is at work, of course, over at the mattress factory in Coopersville, so I'm your welcoming party, key to the city and grand parade all tied up in one package. How was the ride over from Raleigh?

CHARLIE: Okay, I guess.

BERTHA: We're just up the hill a bit. It's kind of steep, but you'll get used to it. 'Course when it rains, it gets a little slippery, with the mud and all. You must be hungry. I hope you like meatloaf, 'cause that's what's on the menu tonight. You might say it's my specialty. Everyone says it's the best meatloaf around. Betty at the beauty shop says I ought to open up a diner and just serve meatloaf, gravy and mashed potatoes...

(Bertha exits speaking, leaving Charlie alone onstage. She opens up her diary as if to write, but soon addresses the audience directly.)

CHARLIE: Dear Diary: I promised that I'd write in you every day as soon as I arrived in Colby, but I honestly don't know where to begin.

(As Charlie's narration continues, lights up briefly on LANIE and BURL in grease-spattered clothes, leaning over the engine of an imaginary car. HOWARD limps across the stage, waving in Charlie's direction.)

Red dirt roads. Sad little patches of grass and gravel in front of every home, and nearly every one has a beat-up car with its hood up out in front of it, like someone was starting to work on it but then gave up and went inside to fix himself a mystery-meat sandwich.

(Musical underscoring [1A]. Lights up on the front porch of Gus and Bertha's house. GUS enters, hoe in hand, appreciating his imaginary garden.)

Gus and Bertha's house hangs over the side of a mountain. It looks like it's about to fall over, if it weren't propped up on stilts. Gus tends the scraggliest little garden you've ever seen but beams over it like it was the Garden of Eden or something. Meanwhile, I keep waiting for the phone to ring. For Mama to call and tell me that she got out of bed that morning and wants me to come home right away.

(Blackout.)

SCENE 2

(Gus and Bertha's front porch. Evening.)

BERTHA: Charlie? Come on out here and sit with us for a spell, would you?

(Charlie enters with her diary.)

What are you doing in there, Charlie?

CHARLIE: Writing in my diary.

BERTHA: You've been here three days, and you haven't told us hardly anything about yourself. Except that you don't like to be called Charlemagne.

CHARLIE: What do you want to know?

BERTHA: Oh, just about everything. Your favorite color. Do you have a lucky number? Do you like boiled peanuts? Why, everyone I know likes boiled peanuts, except for Betty the beautician, but maybe she's the exception that proves the rule. What TV shows do you like to watch? Who's your favorite Bible character?

CHARLIE: *Bible* character?

BERTHA: Mine's Benaiah.

CHARLIE: *Who?*

BERTHA: Benaiah — you know, the one who goes down into a deep, snowy pit and slays a lion with his bare hands.

CHARLIE: Oh. I guess he's mine, too.

BERTHA: Anyways, you're probably telling your diary all about how we put you up in a little room with Mason canning jars and a TV set that doesn't even work. Gus keeps saying he's going to take that set in to get it looked at.

GUS: Well, Bertha, you know that Hank's TV and Radio Shop is only open on weekdays. And Coopersville is clear in the other direction.

BERTHA: I know, Gus. I'm just being impossible. You might think I married Gus for his looks. For he was the handsomest boy in Colby High by far. But I married him for his intellect.

(As if on cue, Gus and Bertha each reach for the other's hand.)

Why, he can tell you everything you ever wanted to know about stars and air and plants and water and weather and all that.

GUS: Up there's the constellation Pegasus.

BERTHA: What did I tell you? But heaven knows what else you're writing about in that diary of yours. Hopefully nothing too terrible. Because with the stars up above our little roof and the ground beneath our feet, we more than get by. Don't we, Gus?

2. Shelves Full of Mason Jars

MAYBE YOU NOTICED WE'RE NOT ROCKEFELLERS
WE DON'T HAVE LOTS OF MONEY
OR FANCY AUTOMOBILES
BUT WE HAVE FOOD UPON THE TABLE
TURNIPS IN THE CELLAR
WE NEVER HAD TO BORROW, OR HAD TO STEAL
WELL, THERE'S NOT A LOT OF ROOM HERE
BUT IT WILL HAVE TO DO,
THAT ROOM THAT WE FIXED UP FOR YOU
SO THOSE SHELVES FULL OF MASON JARS
ARE NOT GOING ANYWHERE, ANYTIME SOON
NO, THOSE SHELVES FULL OF MASON JARS
ARE NOT GOING ANYWHERE, ANYTIME SOON
SPRING FALLS INTO SUMMER, SUMMER INTO FALL

AND THE VINES INSIDE OUR GARDEN
THEY'LL SOON BE GROWING TALL
TOMATOES AND BEANS, THE BEST YOU'VE EVER
TASTED
NOTHING'S EVER WASTED. WE PRESERVE IT ALL
SO THOSE SHELVES FULL OF MASON JARS
ARE NOT GOING ANYWHERE, ANYTIME SOON
NO, THOSE SHELVES FULL OF MASON JARS
ARE NOT GOING ANYWHERE, ANYTIME SOON.

(Music continues until the final measure of the piece.)

Well, I'm turning in, honey. Be sure to let us know if you need anything. By the way, there's Sunday school tomorrow.

CHARLIE: *What?*

BERTHA: Sunday school.

CHARLIE: Don't you have summer vacations around here?

BERTHA: Why, Sunday school will be the best part of your week—at least, that's what the Odom kids always say.

CHARLIE: Who are the Odom kids?

BERTHA: Burl and Lanie and Howard—the finest people you'll ever meet. Just a few weeks ago, Burl and Lanie spent all of a Saturday helping Gus replace some boards on the porch. Of course they wouldn't let us pay them, so I gave them a bag of turnips, and they were so excited, you'd think it was a bag of gold coins. Lanie is the singer in the family. A bit of a tomboy, I guess you can say, but she sings like an angel. Howard's the youngest. He broke his leg when he was about two, and I suppose it was never set right. So he walks a little different, but he doesn't let a little thing like that get in his way, bless his heart. Don't bat an eye when kids poke fun at him, calling him names like Pogo. Anyway, Sunday school is games and songs and acting out Bible stories and making friends, and the time will go by so fast that the morning will be over before you know it. *(Getting ready to exit into the house:)* Well, be sure to turn the porch light off before you turn in.

(Bertha exits, followed by Gus.)

GUS: Good night, Charlie.

CHARLIE: Good night.

(Charlie turns back to her diary, then addresses the audience directly:)

Bertha and Gus are fine and all, but I feel like I've been dumped here like a sack of unwanted kittens. Meanwhile, Jackie will be spending her summer suntanning around the pool and drinking Cherry Cokes and probably never thinking of me at all. And to make matters worse, I just realized that I haven't made my wish today, so I might have to wait until nine minutes after eleven and make it then. I can't skip a day — especially not now.

(Charlie closes her diary. The hooting of an owl. Once, twice.)

Once. Twice. C'mon, owl. One more time, please, and I get to make today's wish and go to bed.

(Another owl hoot.)

There it is. Thank you, owl. So here's today's wish. I'll share it with you and you alone, because even though you're not supposed to tell anyone your wish, telling it to an owl doesn't count. So here's what I wish for today, and each and every day: my family, whole and together and in one piece. All of us taking care of each other. Sometimes, when I close my eyes, I can see it all in front of me, like a beautiful home movie in full color: Mama and Daddy in the front seat of the car, me in the back — Jackie, too, if she's not working at the Waffle House that day.

(Music begins.)

3. <u>One Fine Day</u>

ONE FINE DAY, ONE SUMMER SUNDAY
SUNDAY DRIVING 'NEATH A CLOUDLESS SKY
MAMA'S LOOKING SO FINE
MAKING UP FOR LOST TIME. MAKING UP FOR LOST
TIME.
LUSCIOUS PEACHES ON THE DASHBOARD
SUNLIGHT GLINTING OFF OF DADDY'S EYES
SAYS HE'S DONE WITH THAT JAIL.
GONNA TEACH ME TO SAIL
GONNA TEACH ME TO SAIL
I CAN SEE IT. I CAN HEAR IT.
I CAN FEEL IT GLIDING 'CROSS THAT BAY
GETTING NEARER. GETTING CLEARER.
DADDY STEERS HER AND NOTHING'S IN OUR WAY
ONE FINE DAY, ONE SUNDAY MORNING
WE BOUGHT SOME FLOWERS, FOR WE'VE GOT CLASS.
ALL THAT PAIN'S IN THE PAST
ALWAYS KNEW IT WOULDN'T LAST
IT WOULDN'T LAST

(Blackout. Scene change music [3A].)

SCENE 3

(Lights up on Howard, Burl, Lanie, AUDREY and Charlie, all standing or seated in a row. A TEACHER presides.)

TEACHER: Welcome back to Sunday school, everyone! As you may have noticed, we have a new student who recently moved here from Raleigh—Charlemagne Reese. Welcome, Charlemagne!

AUDREY: Charlemagne? What kind of a name is that?

CHARLIE: It's...the name of a very famous and very wealthy king of France who I'm directly descended from. But since it's so difficult for people to spell, I prefer to be called Charlie.

TEACHER: Okay then, Charlie. Tell us a little more about yourself. What do you most enjoy doing, outside of attending Sunday school—?

AUDREY: And lying.

TEACHER: *(Warning her:)* Audrey.

CHARLIE: *(Eyes shooting daggers at Audrey:)* That would be ballet, soccer and fighting.

TEACHER: *(With a forced laugh:)* Alright! Charlie, honey, since you're new here, you're going to need to have a Bible buddy—someone to show you the ropes.

CHARLIE: I'm probably not going to be here very long, so I actually think I'll be fine without one.

HOWARD: I'll be Charlie's Bible buddy!

(He extends a hand.)

Hi, I'm Howard Odom! I've seen you around town!

CHARLIE: What town?

TEACHER: It's decided then! Howard, why don't you sit down next to Charlie? 'Cause we're going to play Bible detective.

ALL EXCEPT CHARLIE: Yay!

(Vamp begins [4].)

CHARLIE: Bible detective?

HOWARD: It's so much fun, Charlie. And you get to earn Bible bucks.

CHARLIE: Bible bucks?

(Lanie begins to sing:)

<u>4. Bible Bucks</u>

LANIE: WELL, THE GOOD BOOK TELLS OH SO MANY STORIES
OF COURAGE, ENDURANCE AND PLUCK
AND YOU'LL LEARN THEM ALL IN TIME
IF YOUR FORTUNE'S ON THE LINE
'CAUSE YOU'RE PLAYING FOR BIBLE BUCKS.

LANIE, BURL, HOWARD & AUDREY: GONNA EARN ME SOME BIBLE BUCKS
ROCK OF MY SOUL, GONNA SAVE THEM UP
WATCH AS MY SAVINGS START TO GROW
OH! 'CAUSE THERE'S NO ONE MORE DISCERNING
THAN SOMEONE WHO'S BEEN LEARNING
WHILE ADDING UP THOSE BIBLE BUCKS, YOU KNOW

(Vamp continues.)

TEACHER: Let's begin. How many braids were in Samson's hair?

(Howard's arm shoots up.)

Howard.

HOWARD: Samson's hair had seven braids.

TEACHER: Correct. One Bible buck for you, Howard. Okay: what was Moses's brother named?

(Howard's arm shoots up.)

Yes, Howard?

HOWARD: Moses's brother was Aaron!

TEACHER: Howard, honey, you are on fire!

(Vamp continues. As the others silently pantomime the action in dim light, Howard continuing to ace the quiz, Charlie pulls out

her diary and begins to write, then addresses the audience directly.)

CHARLIE: Dear Diary: I'm writing you from Sunday school. Yes, Sunday school, where they're doing some kind of stupid quiz show. If that doesn't sound exciting enough, there was a dog fight this morning in a dirt driveway near Gus and Bertha's house. A small red dog was mixing it up with a brown and black one, skinny as all get-out, fighting over what looked to be a turkey neck, until an old man turned on a garden hose and aimed it full-force at the skinny dog, which took off running. I'm not sure which dog ended up in possession of the turkey neck, but I'm sure I'll be reading all about it in the *Colby Bugle*.

(Music pauses.)

TEACHER: What about you, Charlie? Any ideas? Even Howard seems to be stumped on this one.

CHARLIE: Who's Howard?

HOWARD: *I'm* Howard — your Bible buddy!

CHARLIE: What was the question?

TEACHER: The question was, who slew the lion on a cold, snowy day? With his bare hands.

CHARLIE: Uh...Benaiah?

TEACHER: *(Handing Charlie five bills:)* Why, yes, that's correct! And that answer's worth five Bible bucks, Charlie!

HOWARD: Nice work, Charlie!

CHARLIE: Uh...what can I buy with these, again?

HOWARD: Oh, you can't really buy anything in an actual store. But you can save them and trade them and give them to your friends.

CHARLIE: Here. You can have them. I'm not planning on having any friends in this nowhere town.

AUDREY: I'd say you're off to a very good start, then.

(Lights out on Sunday school. Lights up on Bertha in an undefined space.)

BERTHA: Charlie. Your Sunday school teacher, Mrs. Wallabye, called. She wonders why you stood up in front of the whole class and told them you're descended from royalty.

CHARLIE: What am I supposed to tell them? That Mama spends her days in bed and Scrappy's locked up in the county jail?

(Beat.)

Bertha...

BERTHA: What is it, Charlie? What's on your mind?

CHARLIE: There's a dog out there somewhere. A skinny black and brown dog. I've seen him twice now. He's out there somewhere, and it looks like he's in need of a home.

BERTHA: Oh, that dog. He comes around here every now and then, and whenever I see him, I put out some table scraps for him. He'll eat most anything, but most of all he loves my meatloaf. Why, if I put some meatloaf in a bowl, he'll lick that bowl halfway across the county.

CHARLIE: If I catch him...*when* I catch him, can I keep him?

BERTHA: He's probably full of ticks after living rough for so long. May even have the mange.

CHARLIE: I'd give him a bath.

GUS: *(Entering:)* Even if you catch him, I'm guessing he'll never stay put. He's too used to being a stray. Probably likes it, even.

BERTHA: But you can try to keep him if you catch him, isn't that right, Gus?

GUS: Oh, sure.

BERTHA: Charlie, you didn't say anything about that new Cinderella pillowcase on your bed. When I saw it in the Sears catalogue, I said to myself, "Bertha, that looks just like something that every girl's bedroom needs.'

> *(Bertha and Gus exit. Vamp resumes.)*

CHARLIE: *(Putting on white majorette boots:)* Every five-year-old girl, maybe. I'm eleven.

> *(Charlie joins Howard, Burl, Lanie, Audrey and the Teacher in the space representing the Sunday school again.)*

BURL: WELL, THE GOOD BOOK HAS OH SO MANY PERSONS
AS NUMEROUS AS GRAINS OF SAND
THERE ARE PROPHETS WISE AND GREAT.
JUST TO KEEP THE PROPHETS STRAIGHT
WOULD TRY THE PATIENCE OF WOMAN, SAINT OR MAN

ALL EXCEPT CHARLIE: GONNA EARN ME SOME BIBLE BUCKS
ROCK OF MY SOUL, GONNA SAVE THEM UP
JUST WATCH AS MY SAVINGS START TO GROW
OH! 'CAUSE THERE'S NO ONE MORE DISCERNING
THAN SOMEONE WHO'S BEEN LEARNING
WHILE ADDING UP THOSE BIBLE BUCKS, YOU KNOW

> *(Vamp continues. The Teacher turns her back to write something on an imaginary chalkboard.)*

AUDREY: Nice boots, Charlemagne. Where'd you get them?

CHARLIE: *(Eyes narrowing:)* From my sister.

HOWARD: Charlie. Whenever I feel mad, before I go and do something I may later regret, I make myself say "pineapple" three times.

AUDREY: What do you use 'em for, if you don't mind my asking?

CHARLIE: I use 'em for kicking hillbillies. *(Aside, to Howard:)* Why pineapple?

HOWARD: I don't know! Because it always works. For me, at least.

CHARLIE: And why are you telling me this?

HOWARD: Because I'm your Bible buddy. I'm supposed to be looking out for you.

CHARLIE: Fine, then. Pineapple. Pineapple. Pineapple. *(To Howard:)* I'm gonna need a better word.

(Charlie kicks Audrey in the shin. The Teacher turns around at that moment, her mouth agape.)

AUDREY: Ow! She kicked me! In a house of worship!

(Vamp pauses. Lights out on Sunday school. All exit except for Charlie, diary in hand.)

CHARLIE: *(Writing in her diary, then addressing the audience directly:)* Dear Diary: I think the real reason that I kicked Audrey on that second Sunday wasn't because of her snide question. It had to do with the Garden of Blessings, which came right before Bible bucks. We all had to write something that we felt grateful for on cardboard flowers, and she wrote "My Family" in big, flowery, show-offy cursive, and I couldn't think of anything to write. Anything at all.

(The phone rings.)

Anyway, I had to go over to Audrey's house the next day and apologize, and believe it or not, they kept me in Sunday school. There's apparently no sin so grave that gets you kicked out, except maybe murder and idolatry. Probably not even that. But two more weeks have gone by uneventfully, and another Sunday morning has rolled around. I've gotten to almost like my Bible buddy, Howard. Audrey's not so bad, either.

BERTHA: *(Entering with a phone on a cord:)* Charlie, Jackie's on the phone.

CHARLIE: Hello?

(Lights up on JACKIE on another part of the stage, on the telephone.)

JACKIE: Hi there, Charlie. How's lil' ol' Colby treating you?

CHARLIE: Alright, I guess. I'm just heading out the door to Sunday school.

JACKIE: *Sunday* school?

CHARLIE: What are you doing today?

JACKIE: Oh, it's such a beautiful day, so we're all going to the beach.

CHARLIE: The beach?

JACKIE: You know. Suntan lotion and beach balls and Cherry Cokes and all. 'Course we're gonna stop at the Piggly-Wiggly on our way out of town and pick up everything we need—Carol Lee and her boyfriend and my boyfriend and me.

CHARLIE: You have a boyfriend?

JACKIE: His name is Arlo, and he's really nice.

(Beat.)

Is everything okay, Charlie?

CHARLIE: Yeah. Everything's great. You better head on over to the ocean. I wouldn't want you to miss out on any of those big, beautiful ocean waves. Bye, Jackie. I'll talk to you later.

(Charlie hangs up. Lights out on Jackie.)

BERTHA: Did you and Jackie get caught up a little?

CHARLIE: Well, she's going to the beach today. You know — the Atlantic Ocean. Don't know if you've ever seen it, or even heard of it, since it's way past these hills, about a thousand miles in that direction.

BERTHA: I've heard of it. I'm...not much for talking about feelings and such, Charlie. But I know it must be hard to see your mama lose her way like she has. And to worry about Scrappy. And to miss your sister so. I'm not surprised that you're angry at the way things have worked out —

CHARLIE: Things have not worked out! 'Cause I hate Colby, and all the backwoods kids that live here, and this nasty old house hanging off the side of the mountain, and all those Mason jars in my room. And I especially hate those Cinderella pillowcases you bought me 'cause I'm not five years old, you know. Now, you're making me late for Sunday school. And I'm *not* angry!

(Charlie storms out.)

BERTHA: Oh, Charlie.

(Blackout.)

(The Odoms enter singing, on their way to Sunday school. Lanie and Burl are walking. Howard rides along lazily on his bicycle. Charlie sits sulking a short distance away.)

LANIE: WELL, THE GOOD BOOK HAS SO MANY RHYMES AND REASONS
AND SEASONS AND STORIES SO DIVINE

AND ON THIS YOU CAN DEPEND,
ONCE YOU'VE GOTTEN TO THE END
YOU'LL GO BACK AND READ IT ALL OVER AGAIN

LANIE, BURL & HOWARD: GONNA EARN ME SOME
BIBLE BUCKS
ROCK OF MY SOUL, GONNA SAVE THEM UP
WATCH AS MY SAVINGS START TO GROW
OH—!

(They stop singing when they see Charlie.)

HOWARD: *(Getting off his bicycle:)* Hi, Charlie. Aren't you going to Sunday school?

CHARLIE: Go away.

HOWARD: *(Laying his bicycle on the ground:)* No. What's wrong? You have to tell me what's going on.

CHARLIE: I don't have to tell you anything.

HOWARD: *(To his siblings:)* You two go ahead. I'll catch up.

LANIE: Hope you feel better, Charlie.

BURL: Hope everything's alright.

(Lanie and Burl exit.)

HOWARD: A ladybug just landed on your hand.

CHARLIE: That's the only good thing that's happened to me so far today. It's good for today's wish.

HOWARD: What do you mean? Do you make a wish every day?

CHARLIE: Yes, of course I do. *(Holding her finger up:)* Ladybug, ladybug, fly away home.

HOWARD: What did you just wish for?

CHARLIE: I wished for you to go away. But now it's not going to come true. Because I said it out loud.

HOWARD: Oh, Charlie, you're incorrigible. My mama says you should never keep all your troubles to yourself. She says if you share 'em with somebody, they get smaller.

CHARLIE: I don't care what your mama says.

HOWARD: Did you kick somebody again? Poke 'em with a pencil? Pointy end?

CHARLIE: No!

HOWARD: Mama made this needlepoint sign that says, "If all our troubles were hung on a line, you'd choose yours and I'd choose mine."

CHARLIE: What's that supposed to mean?

HOWARD: It means everyone's got troubles and some of 'em are worse than yours. Or something like that.

CHARLIE: That's a good one, Howard, 'cause I can't think of anybody with worse troubles than me. My father Scrappy and I used to spend our Sundays watching *Wheel of Fortune* and eating macaroni and cheese for breakfast, and now he's in the Wake County Jail. Last time I saw my mama, she was crying into her pillow in her dark bedroom, not caring one little bit whether I had clean clothes or even went to school. Mama and Scrappy would holler at each other all the livelong day while me and my sister Jackie sat on her bed with the radio turned up so we didn't have to hear them. And then Scrappy would drive off with tires screeching and gravel flying every which way while Mama yelled, "Good riddance to bad rubbish" from the front porch. And Jackie and I knew the words to nearly every song on the radio, and she would French braid my hair and share her nail polish with me, and I miss her every single day, even though her life is a thousand times better than mine and she's going to the beach today—the Atlantic Ocean! And then I go on and yell at Bertha and say the most awful things to her, when I know deep down that she and Gus are only trying to be good to me. So try hanging those troubles on a clothesline.

> *(Beat.)*

HOWARD: Want my advice?

CHARLIE: I guess. Sure. I don't know.

HOWARD: You can't do nothing about Scrappy and your mom back in Raleigh or Jackie having a life that's a thousand times better than yours. The only thing you can fix is what you done to Bertha.

> *(WISHBONE appears at the edge of the woods. Musical underscoring [4A].)*

CHARLIE: *(Whispering:)* Shhhh! Don't move.

> *(Wishbone regards Charlie, head tilted to one side, tail wagging.)*

> *(Calling him softly:)* Wishbone.

HOWARD: Wishbone?

CHARLIE: That's his name.

HOWARD: How do you know?

CHARLIE: Because I just made it up. Come here, fella. Come here, boy. My Aunt Bertha tells me that you're fond of meatloaf. *(Approaching the dog:)* Hey, fella.

> *(The sound of a car horn and a car roaring by. Wishbone, startled, runs off.)*

Dang it!

HOWARD: I must have seen that dog a dozen times before. He's a stray.

CHARLIE: He's mine—he just doesn't know it yet. He's a fighter like me.

(Beat.)

Aren't you going to say, "What do you want with a stray dog who's probably full of ticks and mange"?

HOWARD: There's only one person in the world who can tell you what you want. And that's you.

CHARLIE: Or maybe you're going to say, "Gee, Charlie, that dog is probably happy as he is, being a stray."

HOWARD: No. I don't know what's going to make that dog happy or not, so why would I say a thing like that?

CHARLIE: You go on now. Go on to Sunday school. I've got something more important to do back home.

HOWARD: Okay. See you later, Charlie.

(Howard gets back on his bike and rides away, sounding his bell. Blackout.)

(The front porch. Lights up on Bertha, her back turned. Charlie enters, hesitates for a long beat, then speaks.)

CHARLIE: I'm sorry, Bertha.

(Bertha turns to face Charlie.)

I didn't mean to holler at you. And I don't actually hate this house perched on this mountainside with the piney woods all around us. And those Mason jars don't bother me one little bit. And I don't mind Cinderella that much, either. So I hope you're not too sore at me.

(Gus enters. Bertha looks into Charlie's eyes.)

BERTHA: Tomorrow is another day. And I'm not sore at you. Not at all. Gus and I, we just want you to be happy here. We haven't had any practice being parents, Charlie. But I hope you'll be patient with us while we learn.

CHARLIE: I'll try.

GUS: Bertha, what do you say we have some of that blackberry cobbler before lunch?

BERTHA: *Before* lunch? Why, Gus, you're just as wild now as the day I met you!

> (*Bertha and Gus hug affectionately. Charlie, not used to such a sight, looks on with bemused curiosity. Day turns to evening. The sky darkens, and the stars appear.*)

> (*Howard appears, flashlight in hand, and knocks at the door. Bertha answers.*)

Howard, what are you doing here this time of night? Is something wrong?

HOWARD: No, ma'am, but I wonder if I might have a few words with Charlie. It's very important.

BERTHA: Charlie! It's Howard. He wants to talk with you.

CHARLIE: (*Stepping out onto the porch:*) Hi, Howard. What is it?

HOWARD: I just wanted you to know that I asked my mother to make meatloaf for supper tonight. I'm sure it's nowhere near as tasty as the meatloaf that your Aunt Bertha makes, but we at the Odom house have always liked it just fine.

CHARLIE: I'm sure it's delicious. Is that what you came over to tell me?

HOWARD: Well, actually there was something else.

> (*Musical underscoring [4B].*)

After dinner, I put some in a bowl out by the shed and sat and waited for it—must have been an hour or two—and sure enough, who didn't stop by but that stray dog that you call Wishbone. And we were all ready this time—me and Lanie and Burl—with a collar and a rope, and it didn't take more than a minute to catch him and calm him down, and wouldn't you know it, he's the friendliest dog you ever laid eyes on—

CHARLIE: You *have* him?

HOWARD: They're all right there, at the end of your driveway—Lanie and Burl and Wishbone!

(*Blackout.*)

SCENE 4

(*Bright musical intro. Lights up on Charlie's room. A narrow bed with a Cinderella pillowcase, Mason jars on shelves. Wishbone has made himself comfortable on the bed.*)

(*Anytime Charlie speaks to Wishbone, he responds expressively.*)

<u>5. With a Dog Like You</u>

CHARLIE: Good morning, Wishbone. How'd you sleep? I know you didn't care much for that flea bath last night, but I have to say, you do smell a lot better. Well, are you ready for some adventures today?

WE'VE GOT SOME CATCHING UP TO DO
BUT FROM THE FIRST MOMENT I SAW YOU
I JUST KNEW WE'D BE LIKE TOAST AND JAM.
DO YOU LIKE THE SOUND OF YOUR NAME?
WHAT DO YOU THINK OF BURIED TREASURES,
SIMPLE PLEASURES, COMPLICATED PLANS?
GONNA PAINT YOUR STURDY TOENAILS RED
AND OF COURSE YOU GET TO SLEEP ON MY BED
'CAUSE WITH A DOG LIKE YOU
THIS STORY HAS A NEW BEGINNING
IT'S WEARING STORE-BOUGHT SHOES

IT'S A GAME THAT'S GONE TO EXTRA INNINGS.
AND IF CHASING RABBITS IS YOUR HABIT
THEN I SUPPOSE THAT I CAN LET THAT SLIDE
TO HAVE A DOG LIKE YOU
ALWAYS BY MY SIDE

>*(Music continues.)*

Now, I hope you're not counting on staying in Colby your whole doggone life, because we're only here temporarily.

ONCE MAMA'S FINALLY FOUND HER WAY
WE'LL BE PICKING UP AND MOVING BACK TO RALEIGH
CARS AND TROLLEYS, PEOPLE, SIGHTS AND SOUNDS
AT FIRST SHE'S APT TO BE A BIT RILED
BUT SOONER OR LATER SHE'LL COME AROUND
TO THE BENEFITS OF HAVING A FINE HOUND.
GONNA TEACH YOU HOW TO SIT AND STAY
AND HOW TO KEEP THOSE SOCIAL WORKERS AWAY

>*(Music continues.)*

BERTHA: *(Entering with a phone on a cord:)* Charlie. Your sister Jackie's on the phone.

CHARLIE: Hi, Jackie. Is everything alright?

>*(Lights up on Jackie, talking on the phone.)*

JACKIE: Every little thing is just fine here! You know, when I got off the phone the other day, I realized how much I missed you.

CHARLIE: Oh, I miss you, too. I've got a dog now, Jackie! Someone to keep me company!

JACKIE: A dog?! Why, that's wonderful. Anyway, I've just been talking to Aunt Bertha, and I'll be coming out there to Colby for a visit in just about a week.

CHARLIE: For real?!

JACKIE: Can't wait to see you, honey.

CHARLIE: Oh, me neither, Jackie.

JACKIE: Well, this is a long-distance call, so I better sign off.

CHARLIE: Bye, Jackie!

(Charlie hangs up. Lights out on Jackie.)

(To Wishbone:) You're going to like my sister—I just know you will. She's a lot like me, except a little older and maybe a little prettier. Well, enough yapping for now. Let's go have some breakfast and go outdoors to see what my buddy Howard is up to.

'CAUSE WITH A DOG LIKE YOU
THIS STORY HAS A NEW BEGINNING
IT'S WEARING STORE-BOUGHT SHOES
IT'S A GAME THAT'S GONE TO EXTRA INNINGS.
AND IF CHASING RABBITS IS YOUR HABIT
I SUPPOSE THAT I CAN TAKE THAT IN STRIDE
TO HAVE A DOG LIKE YOU
ALWAYS BY MY SIDE. MY SIDE. MY SIDE.
MY SIDE. MY SIDE.

(Blackout.)

SCENE 5

(The sounds of a woodland, with a nearby creek. Howard enters, followed by Charlie. Wishbone ranges every which way, following each interesting scent and sound.)

HOWARD: They call this place Miller's Creek, but no one seems to know why. Wishbone seems to like it here just fine. 'Course, he must know these woods even better than I do.

CHARLIE: He's going to like Raleigh, too, when we go back.

HOWARD: When are you going back?

CHARLIE: Any day now, I suppose. Just as soon as my mama finds her way again. We've got a great big backyard with one of those nice cedar fences around it— *(She stops herself.)*

HOWARD: What is it?

CHARLIE: I don't know why I keep telling stories like that. We've got a tiny little postcard-sized patch of gravel with a chain-link fence, with one post that's actually missing.

HOWARD: It's not a terrible thing to tell a tall tale from time to time—as long as you don't start believing in them yourself.

(A splash.)

HOWARD & CHARLIE: Look at him!

HOWARD: Trying to catch some minnows, it looks like.

CHARLIE: Hook pinkies. Quick!

HOWARD: What?

CHARLIE: We both get to wish. If two people say the same thing at the exact same time, they hook pinkies and make a wish. Jackie taught me that.

(They hook pinkies and stand together for a moment, eyes closed. Then they open their eyes.)

HOWARD: You know a lot about wishing, don't you?

CHARLIE: I've been wishing for the same thing for as long as I can remember, so I've had a lot of practice at it.

HOWARD: Can you teach me what you know? So I can be really good at it.

CHARLIE: Well, to teach you *everything* I know would take some time, I'm afraid. But the first thing to remember is that there are all kinds of things in the world that you can wish upon—and not just four-leaf clovers, falling stars and yellow railroad cars.

HOWARD: Yellow railroad cars?

6. Wish

CHARLIE: Definitely. In fact, I'm usually able to find something to wish on every day.

IF YOU SEE THREE SPARROWS PERCHED ON A WIRE
OR CRIMSON ROSES NESTLED IN A BRIER,
THE WORLD IS SAYING, "WISH YOUR HEART'S DESIRE"
THE POINTY END OF A WARM BERRY PIE
A CART OR WAGON, HAY STACKED HIGH
SOME THINGS JUST EXIST SO WE MAY WISH
AND YOU GET ONE FREE WISH ON THE SECOND DAY
OF SPRING
BUT ONLY IF A CARDINAL'S ON THE WING
AND IF YOU SEE FOUR HORSES STANDING IN THE MIST
AND RAIN,
YOU GET TO WISH AGAIN, AGAIN, AGAIN.
ELEVEN O-NINE COMES TWICE EVERY DAY.
IT'S THE WISHING TIME, SO DON'T LET IT GET AWAY.
CERTAIN RULES EXIST SO WE MIGHT WISH
ONLY SO THAT WE MIGHT WISH

(Music continues.)

Of course, there's the most basic and important rule of all.

HOWARD: What's that?

CHARLIE: Never tell anyone your wish, or else it won't ever come true.

HOWARD: Oh, everyone knows that one, Charlie.

CHARLIE: Well, you'd be surprised at how many people forget that one. And then their wishes never come true. Now, let's see if you remember some of the other rules.

HOWARD: I might need your help!

CHARLIE: Sure, that's okay!

HOWARD: YOU GET ONE WISH EARLY IN SPRING

CHARLIE: THAT'S ONLY IF A CARDINAL'S ON THE WING

HOWARD: ELEVEN O-NINE IS ALWAYS THE BEST TIME

CHARLIE: BIRDS ON WIRES ARE COMMON TO SEE

HOWARD: BUT TO MAKE A WISH, THOSE BIRDIES MUST BE THREE CHIRPING SPARROWS STANDING IN A LINE

CHARLIE & HOWARD: ALL AROUND US, EVERY SINGLE DAY
ARE CHANCES TO WISH
DON'T LET THEM GET AWAY
SOME THINGS JUST EXIST SO WE MAY WISH

CHARLIE: ONLY SO THAT WE

HOWARD: ONLY SO THAT WE

CHARLIE & HOWARD: ONLY SO THAT WE MIGHT WISH!

(Blackout. Scene change music [6A].)

SCENE 6

(Lights up on Charlie, Bertha, Gus and Wishbone by the side of the road.)

GUS: I bet you're excited to see your big sister, Butterbean.

CHARLIE: I surely am. But Uncle Gus, I was wondering: could you please not call me Butterbean in front of Jackie?

GUS: Why sure, honey, if that's what you'd like.

CHARLIE: Oh, there's the bus now!

(The sounds of a bus stopping, then pulling away. Jackie enters, suitcase in hand, stylish and glamorous.)

Jackie, over here!

JACKIE: Why, hello, everybody! Charlie, look at you! I'd say that mountain living is agreeing with you just fine.

BERTHA: *(Extending a hand:)* I'm your Aunt Bertha, and this is your Uncle Gus. Now, I don't much believe in hugging folks I've never before met, even if they are family —

JACKIE: Oh fiddlesticks, Aunt Bertha. I'm going to give both of you the biggest hugs that you've ever seen!

GUS: I'll take that suitcase, Jackie. Butterbean, why don't you grab her satchel, and we'll head on up the hill.

CHARLIE: You're even prettier than I remembered.

JACKIE: Oh, it hasn't been that long, honey! Just four or five weeks. And this must be your new friend —

CHARLIE: Wishbone.

JACKIE: Wishbone! Between you and your wishes, I should have guessed. What a cutie. Hello, Wishbone! Oh, we're all going to have so much fun! I just know it! Now, how about a nice big hug, Charlie? Why, sure! You too, Wishbone!

(Blackout. Scene change music [6B].)

SCENE 7

(The front porch. Morning. Bertha and Jackie's voices are heard from within the house.)

(Lanie and Burl, dressed in their finest garb, approach nervously. Burl's hair is combed neatly for once.)

BERTHA: *(Off:)* I hope that that mattress on the floor weren't too uncomfortable, Jackie.

JACKIE: *(Off:)* I slept like a baby on that little ol' mattress. Don't you worry.

(Lanie and Burl are finally at the door, standing there awkwardly for a moment, each one trying to get the other one to knock.)

BERTHA: *(Off:)* Now, where s that skirt of yours that needs a new zipper? I'll show you exactly how it's done.

(Burl knocks on the door. Off:)

Who could that be? *(Opening the door and stepping onto the porch:)* Why, Lanie and Burl, what a nice surprise. What can I do for the two of you?

(During the conversation, Burl keeps craning his neck, hoping to catch a glimpse of Jackie.)

LANIE: Well, ma'am, we just came by to see how the repairs were holding on this porch of yours.

BURL: Once Howard informed us that one additional person had taken up temporary residence here, I declared that we should come by and make sure the porch was safe for additional inhabitants.

LANIE: And I readily agreed.

BERTHA: The porch seems to be nice and solid. Thank you for checking.

BURL: I see. Well, we was also wondering if you needed any help with anything else around the property. 'Cause we have a few rare hours of leisure time and would be most delighted to be of assistance.

BERTHA: That's so kind of you, Burl. Gus has gone to town, and I can't think of anything that needs fixing, but why don't you two stay for lunch as long as you're here?

LANIE: Oh, we don't mean to impose—

BURL: But as long as we're here, we'll accept your kind offer of hospitality.

JACKIE: *(Stepping out onto the porch:)* Hi there! I'm Jacqueline. But most folks call me Jackie.

(A beat as Burl reacts, starstruck.)

BURL: Uh...pleased to meet you, Miss Jacqueline. I'm Lanie, but most folks call me Howard—

LANIE: What he means to say is he's Burl and I'm Lanie. We're Howard's brother and sister.

BURL: If we appear a little flustered, I guess it's 'cause we never before met someone who looks exactly like Miss America.

JACKIE: Miss America?! Oh, that's too kind—although I *was* crowned Tyson Foods Broiler Queen at the county fair last summer. But I'm really just a waitress at the Waffle House.

LANIE: Well, Tyson Broiler Queen sounds like a great honor indeed, and the Waffle House must be a very fancy, exclusive establishment.

JACKIE: Oh, it's not that fancy, to tell you the truth. Although one time this old lady came in a limo driven by a chauffeur. Can you imagine going to the Waffle House in a chauffeur-driven limo?

BURL: That's difficult for me to imagine. Not that I've ever seen a limousine—outside of a funeral home, maybe.

JACKIE: But she left me a twenty-dollar tip on a four-dollar waffle, so I'm not complaining.

BURL & LANIE: Twenty dollars!

JACKIE: If you two ever get over to Raleigh, you'll have to stop by the restaurant. *(With a wink:)* I'll have the cook put extra chocolate chips in your waffles —

BURL & LANIE: Alright!

JACKIE: Just so long as the manager's not looking, of course. Now, when he's not around and there aren't any customers nearby, we waitresses actually don't call it the Waffle House, but the Awful House.

> *(Burl and Lanie hoot and holler as if this was the funniest thing they'd ever heard. Jackie laughs along. Burl turns to the audience to sing:)*

7. Carolina Angel, Jacqueline

BURL: WELL, HER SMILE'S LIKE A WARM DAY IN
SUMMER
AFTER THE SHOWERS OF MAY
AND THE HALO THAT HOVERS ABOVE HER
CAN CHASE ALL THE CLOUDS CLEAR AWAY.
WELL, THE STORIES SHE TELLS ARE AMUSING.
OF THESE TALES ONE WOULD NOT EVER TIRE.
SHE CAN TELL ANY TALE OF HER CHOOSING
'TIL THE DAY THAT I SADLY EXPIRE.
JACQUELINE IS WHO I MEAN
PURTIEST SIGHT THAT I'VE SEEN
I COULD TRAVEL 'ROUND THE WORLD
BUT NEVER FIND A GIRL,
NOT EVEN ON THE SILVER SCREEN,
LIKE JACQUELINE, THAT BEAUTY QUEEN
FINEST SIGHT THAT THIS TOWN'S EVER SEEN.
MUST HAVE FALLEN FROM A STAR,
AND THE BRIGHTEST ONE BY FAR,
THIS CAROLINA ANGEL, JACQUELINE

(Music continues. Charlie and Wishbone enter.)

JACKIE: By the way, what do frogs order in restaurants?

CHARLIE: Oh, Jackie, not that old joke again! It's not even funny.

BURL: *(Ignoring Charlie:)* What? What do they order in restaurants?

JACKIE: French flies!

(More laughter and hooting.)

BURL: How come you never told us you had a sister, Charlie?

CHARLIE: I musta mentioned my sister to the two of you about a hundred times.

BURL: Yeah, but you never told us that you had this kind of a sister!

LANIE: OH, SHE'S CHARMING, DISARMING AND WINNING
BEGUILING AND STYLISH AND SMART.
NO WONDER THIS POOR BOY IS SINGING
'CAUSE SHE'S PLAYED ALL THE STRINGS
OF HIS HEART

(Music continues. Burl and Jackie dance for four measures.)

CHARLIE: Look at them, Wishbone. Burl all moon-eyed and beside himself. And Lanie seems just about as smitten as Burl.

(Jackie changes partners and dances with Lanie for another four measures.)

BURL & LANIE: JACQUELINE. THAT'S WHO WE MEAN
SPARKLY AS A TAMBOURINE
SHOULD YOU TRAVEL 'ROUND THE WORLD,
YOU'D NEVER FIND A GIRL
NOT EVEN ON THE SILVER SCREEN,

LIKE JACQUELINE, THAT BEAUTY QUEEN
PURTIEST SIGHT THAT THIS COUNTY HAS SEEN
MUST HAVE FALLEN FROM A STAR,
AND THE BRIGHTEST ONE BY FAR,
AND SOMEHOW MISPLACED HER DANG WINGS
SHE'S A CAROLINA ANGEL, JACQUELINE!

(Lights out on Burl, Lanie and Jackie.)

CHARLIE: This week since Jackie arrived has just flown by, Dear Diary: On the night before she was fixing to return to Raleigh, she and I and the Odoms all piled into Gus's pickup truck for a trip to Taste-E-Freeze.

(Blackout. Scene change music [7A].)

SCENE 8

(Charlie and Jackie are seated on a bench finishing their cones outside a Taste-E-Freeze restaurant. The Odoms are on a different zone of the stage.)

JACKIE: How come you never told me you had a Taste-E-Freeze just ten miles down the road from Colby? 'Cause sometimes you get a craving for a soft-serve vanilla cone with chocolate topping and extra Jim-Jims, and nothing else will really do, you know? *(Humming in appreciation:)* Mm, mmm. I've had just a beautiful time here in Colby. With you and Bertha and Gus and the Odoms. And Wishbone, of course.

CHARLIE: Each and every one of us is gonna miss you when you leave tomorrow, Jackie. Burl more than most, I expect. Speaking of which...

(Burl approaches Jackie. Lanie stands close by for support.)

BURL: Jackie. Charlie. Excuse me for interrupting.

JACKIE: What is it, Burl?

BURL: Well...I've always been a great believer in long and leisurely courtships, but since you're departing tomorrow...well, I'm just going to come out and say it. Jacqueline Reese, will you marry me?

(Suddenly remembering, Burl falls to one knee. An awkward pause.)

LANIE: Once you're a member of the Odom family, there's no end to the things we'll be able to learn from each other, Jackie. You can teach me all about the womanly arts of high fashion and makeup and gourmet cuisine and the like, and I can show you how to take apart and rebuild a transmission in no time flat.

JACKIE: Why, Burl. Lanie. Thank you! Golly, I'm flattered. But if I were to marry you, Burl, it would break my poor boyfriend's heart. So I'm afraid I'm going to have to decline.

BURL: Oh, that's okay, Jackie.

LANIE: We just thought we'd ask.

JACKIE: You're really dear, Burl. And you too, Lanie. And we'll always be the best of friends, I hope.

BURL: Sure we will, Jackie. You bet we will.

(Burl and Lanie walk off.)

JACKIE: *(Sympathetically:)* Ohhh. I think I broke his heart a little.

CHARLIE: Oh, I know you did. But he'll come around soon, so long as he has a broken-down jalopy to work on.

JACKIE: I'll miss you like crazy, Charlie.

(Beat.)

What is it, honey? What's on your mind?

CHARLIE: Can you take us back to Raleigh with you, Jackie? Wishbone and me.

(Beat.)

You're not answering. You had better answer, because this silence is about to swallow me up. Maybe Mama's gotten better —

JACKIE: Oh, Charlie. Do you know that Mama left us when we were little? Just ran off with a garbage bag full of clothes to start a new life? She came back after a while, of course, but I still remember that. How can a child ever again trust a mama who does something like that?

(Beat.)

You know what Bertha said to me earlier today?

CHARLIE: What?

JACKIE: "Jackie," she said, "Gus and I want you to know that you'll always have family here. A place to come home to whenever you want." Hearing that was worth more to me than all the swimming pools and Cherry Cokes in the world. It made me cry a little bit, too.

(Musical underscoring begins [7B].)

You got a good life here, Charlie. You got Gus and Bertha loving you and treating you like a princess. You got all those Odoms thanking the good Lord for you. And that Howard is the nicest friend you could ever want. You got these beautiful mountains and a garden and a porch to sit on that's like sitting on the side of heaven. And a dog that loves you like nobody's business. Don't hate me, Charlie.

CHARLIE: I don't hate you, Jackie. If I had more practice saying it, I would say just the opposite. "I love you," is what I'd say — if only I had more practice. And yes, it's not altogether bad here, especially since Wishbone came into my life. But I just keep thinking and wishing about home, about us all being together again—the same as it was, but better. Everyone all better, and happy—our family.

JACKIE: Oh, don't you see? That little ol' family of ours is a lost cause.

8. Nothing's Gonna Change

MAMA'S GONNA KEEP ON BEING MAMA
SCRAPPY'S GONNA KEEP ON BEING SCRAPPY
EACH OF THEM IS FULLY GROWN
YOU AND I ARE ON OUR OWN
NOTHING'S GONNA CHANGE
NOTHING'S GONNA EVER CHANGE
JUST LIKE YOU, I THOUGHT IT WOULD
ALWAYS THOUGHT IT SHOULD
BUT IT ALL STAYED THE SAME
WISHING CAN BE FINE
IF THAT'S HOW YOU WANT TO SPEND YOUR DAY
I KNOW HOW MUCH YOU LOVE YOUR WISHING
SO I'D NEVER WANT TO TAKE THAT AWAY
BUT IF YOU LET YOUR DREAMS
RUN WILD AND FREE
LIKE AN UNTAMED RIVER TO THE OPEN SEA
THEY MIGHT JUST TELL YOU WHO YOU REALLY ARE
AND WHO YOU'RE TRYING TO BE
FOR ONCE YOUR HEART CAN SEE
THEN EVERYTHING CAN CHANGE
CAN'T SAY WHERE AND REALLY DON'T KNOW WHEN
COULD BE IN THE DISTANT FUTURE
OR JUST AROUND THE BEND
BUT HOLD THIS NOTION FAST:
SOMETHING'S GONNA CHANGE AT LAST

SOMETHING'S GONNA CHANGE AT LAST

(Blackout. Scene change music [8A].)

SCENE 9

(The front porch. Night. Distant thunder. The sound of thrashing in the woods. Wishbone barks, appears on the porch, then exits off in the direction of the noise. After a beat, Charlie appears in a bathrobe, followed by Bertha and Gus, also in nightwear. Gus has a flashlight.)

CHARLIE: Wishbone! Wishbone, come back here!

BERTHA: What happened?

CHARLIE: I heard something thrashing about in the woods, and then Wishbone just took off after it, like greased lightning. Wishbone! Come back home, now!

GUS: Hmm. We had a mountain lion prowling around here awhile back, but we figured she had moved on—

CHARLIE: A mountain lion?! *Wishbone!*

BERTHA: Could have been a raccoon or possum or heaven knows what, don't you think, Gus?

GUS: Yep, I suppose.

CHARLIE: I'm worried, Gus and Bertha.

BERTHA: That Wishbone knows how to take care of himself. He'll be back, Charlie.

(The scene continues in pantomime—Gus walking the property, flashlight in hand, calling for the dog.)

CHARLIE: *(Addressing the audience directly:)* Dear Diary: Two days have gone by, and Wishbone's still missing! The Odoms are still off in Tennessee visiting family, but the three of us have been looking everywhere, and with each passing hour I'm losing hope of ever seeing him again.

(Daylight. Charlie moves to the porch step and sits there, despondent, her chin resting on her hands. The sound of Howard's bike bell. Howard enters.)

HOWARD: I came over as soon as I heard the news that Wishbone ran off. I'll help you look for him!

CHARLIE: We've looked everywhere, Howard—for two days! It's hopeless.

HOWARD: No, it's not!

CHARLIE: I guess that all along that dog never wanted to be anything other than a stray.

HOWARD: I don't believe that. He loves you, Charlie. On the way over here, I saw a yellow railroad car on the Norfolk Southern tracks.

CHARLIE: So?

HOWARD: I made a wish that he'd return. I know that you're not supposed to say your wish out loud, but sometimes you just have to!

(Beat.)

It was a yellow railroad car, Charlie!

(Musical underscoring [8B].)

CHARLIE: All those things I told you about wishing—they're just all made up. They're dumb superstitions for people who haven't grown up.

HOWARD: No—don't say that. Wishing is part of who you are.

CHARLIE: Not anymore it's not. I've decided to say goodbye to all of my wishes, the wishes I put out there, and tell them not to bother to come back home.

HOWARD: No, Charlie—

CHARLIE: And maybe you should do the same. I'm pretty sure I know what your one true, everyday wish is—that you're going to wake up one day and not have that up-down walk of yours. But that's never going to happen, so you might as well grow up, too, and stop wishing for it.

(Bertha appears at the screen door, unnoticed by Charlie and Howard.)

HOWARD: You're wrong about my wish. I know very well that no amount of wishing can take away this old walk of mine. My wish...was something different. It was that we could always be friends.

(Howard turns and begins to walk away.)

CHARLIE: Howard. I'm sorry. I'm just really upset.

HOWARD: *(Turning back:)* So am I!

CHARLIE: *(Standing up:)* Upset about Jackie leaving and Wishbone running off and realizing that my family is never, ever going to be set right. Next time, when I'm upset, I'm gonna try to remember to say something different—pineapple or mountain bluebird or something. But the truth is, coming to this sorry old hillbilly town was a big mistake from the start. The truth is, I wish...I had never set foot in Colby.

HOWARD: I can't talk to you any more right now. Goodbye, Charlie.

BERTHA: *(Stepping out onto the porch, heartbroken:)* Howard...Charlie...

HOWARD: Good afternoon, ma'am.

(Howard bikes away.)

CHARLIE: I want to go back to Raleigh, please. I know that you and Gus have tried very hard, but I can't stay here anymore. If you try to keep me here, I'm just going to run away. Maybe I'm incorrigible—like Mama and Scrappy. *(Handing Bertha a page torn from her diary:)* Here.

BERTHA: What's this?

CHARLIE: I want to go back east and take my chances with another placement. Even if it's no better than this one, at least I'll have my sister nearby. So please call Miss Reynolds, the social worker, and tell her what I've decided. Please. Now, if it's alright with you, I'm going to my room.

(Charlie exits into the house as Bertha collapses into a porch chair.)

(Blackout. Scene change music [8C].)

SCENE 10

(Lights up on Charlie sitting by the creek the next day, absently throwing pebbles. She hears Howard's bicycle bell. Howard enters with a large sheet of paper.)

HOWARD: Hi.

CHARLIE: Hi. What are you doing here?

HOWARD: Looking for you.

CHARLIE: What for?

HOWARD: Because that's what a friend does.

CHARLIE: I don't know why you would want anything to do with me after I hurt your feelings so.

HOWARD: We all say dumb things sometimes. Besides, you said you were sorry.

CHARLIE: I'm very, *very* sorry.

(*Beat.*)

I'm going back to Raleigh. The social worker said she'd find me another placement closer to home if I was unhappy here — and I am. I'm unhappy here.

HOWARD: What's going to happen to Bertha and Gus?

CHARLIE: What do you mean?

HOWARD: They love you, Charlie.

CHARLIE: Love me?

HOWARD: Bertha has the biggest heart — and it's just full of love for you. She just isn't that good at showing her feelings.

CHARLIE: What's that you have?

HOWARD: Just a big piece of butcher block paper and a couple of pens.

CHARLIE: What are you going to do with it?

HOWARD: It's what we're going to do together — to try and find Wishbone before you go on and leave town.

9. Let's Draw a Map

LET'S DRAW A MAP, CHARLIE
LET'S MAKE A PLAN.
A WAGON GOES NOWHERE
IF ITS WHEELS ARE STUCK IN SAND.
TWO HEADS TOGETHER, FOUR CAPABLE HANDS.
LET'S DRAW AN EXCELLENT MAP.
I'LL DRAW THE HOUSES,
THE GRAVEL AND LAWNS.
YOU DRAW THE BROKEN-DOWN CARS.
I'LL DRAW THE HILLS,
THE STREAMS AND THE FAWNS.

YOU CAN DRAW THE STARS.
YOU DRAW THE WEST SIDE
I'LL DRAW THE EAST.
BY NOW YOU KNOW THIS TOWN
SO AT THE VERY LEAST
WHY DON'T WE TRY IT?
'CAUSE NOTHING'S OUT OF REACH
LET'S DRAW AN EXCELLENT MAP

    (Music continues.)

I brought you something else.

CHARLIE: What is it?

HOWARD: The pointy end of my mom's cherry pie.

    (Beat.)

I still believe in wishing, Charlie, even if you don't, and I'm going to wish for Wishbone to come home, and then we can both have a bite. But I don't think we ought to stop there.

I'LL DRAW THE HOUSES,
THE GRAVEL AND LAWNS.
YOU DRAW THE BROKEN-DOWN CARS.
I'LL DRAW THE HILLS,
THE STREAMS AND THE FAWNS.
YOU CAN DRAW THE STARS.
YOU DRAW THE WEST SIDE
I'LL DRAW THE EAST.
WORKING TOGETHER
WE'RE BOUND TO TAME THIS BEAST.
WHY DON'T WE TRY IT?
'CAUSE NOTHING'S OUT OF REACH
LET'S DRAW AN EXCELLENT MAP
LET'S DRAW AN EXCELLENT MAP

    (Blackout. Scene change music [9A].)

SCENE 11

(Lights up on Bertha at the Beauty Shop, represented by a chair and a vintage wall calendar. BETTY the beautician places an old-fashioned dryer-curler over Bertha's head.)

BETTY: I hear tell that Charlie is fixing to go back to Raleigh.

BERTHA: As soon as they find another home for her. 'Course, we thought she'd like it here. But with youngsters, I guess there's no telling sometimes —

(Lanie and Burl rush in, the bells on the door jingling.)

Lanie and Burl, what is it?

LANIE: We saw you underneath this flying saucer contraption and decided we ought to make sure you was okay and not being held against your will by aliens.

BETTY: This is just one of those new twentieth-century hair dryers, kids.

LANIE: Oh, that's a relief, ma'am.

BURL: Well, we best be on our way, then. We're looking for that ol' dog Wishbone.

BERTHA: I know that Howard and Charlie drew up a map of the entire town —

LANIE: Which is all well and good, but what if ol' Wishbone decided not to stay within the town limits but instead wandered off into the mountains or down into the river valley?

10. Where You Gone To, Wishbone?

WHERE YOU GONE TO, WISHBONE,
YOU SCRAWNY LITTLE HOUND?
WE'VE BEEN UP THE HILLS AND O'ER THE DALE
AND YER NOWHERE TO BE FOUND

BURL: BUT THIS SEARCH IS NOT YET OVER
HECK, IT'S JUST BEGUN
THERE'S SO DOGGONE MANY PLACES 'NEATH THE SUN

LANIE AND BURL: THAT'S WHY WE'D REALLY LIKE TO
KNOW
MISTER WISHBONE, WHERE'D YOU RUN?

(Music continues. All exit except for Betty, who turns over a day on the wall calendar. Audrey enters in a hurry, holding a flyer with Wishbone's mug shot printed on it.)

AUDREY: Morning, Betty. You ain't see this lil' ol' dog Wishbone, have you?

BETTY: No, but you can bet that I've been keeping an eye out for him, though.

AUDREY: Well, thank you for that!

(As Audrey sings, the Ensemble enters.)

WHERE YOU GONE TO, WISHBONE,
WHEREVER CAN YOU BE?
WAS YOU CHASIN' SOME OL' PESKY SQUIRREL
AND END UP IN A TREE?
WELL, THE GAL OR GUY WHO FINDS YOU
IS GONNA BE IN LUCK
THERE'S A BIG REWARD OF A HUNDRED BIBLE BUCKS!
THIS WHOLE DANG TOWN WOULD LIKE TO KNOW
MISTER WISHBONE, WHERE'D YOU RUN?

ENSEMBLE: WHERE YOU GONE TO, WISHBONE?
WHERE YOU GONE TO, WISHBONE?
WHERE YOU GONE TO, WISHBONE?

(Music continues. Audrey, Lanie and Burl dance.)

(Betty turns over another day on her calendar, then exits.)

(Lights up on Gus behind a steering wheel.)

GUS: WHERE YOU GONE TO, WISHBONE,
YOU SCRAWNY LITTLE DOG?
'CAUSE WE'VE BEEN LOOKING EVERYWHERE
THROUGH RAIN AND SUN AND FOG

> *(Lanie and Betty pop up from behind Gus, apparently along for the ride.)*

LANIE & BETTY: WE'VE BEEN SEARCHING LOW AND HIGH
FROM THE BOULDERS TO THE TREES
NEAR ALL THE WAY TO EASTERN TENNESSEE
AND SO WE'D REALLY LIKE TO KNOW
MISTER WISHBONE, WHERE'D YOU RUN?

ENSEMBLE: WHERE YOU GONE TO, WISHBONE?
WHERE YOU GONE TO, WISHBONE?
WHERE YOU GONE TO, WISHBONE?

> *(The Ensemble switches to a cappella.)*

WHERE YOU GONE TO, WISHBONE?
WHERE YOU GONE TO, WISHBONE?
WHERE YOU GONE TO, WISHBONE—?

CHARLIE: *(Stepping out onto the front porch:)* Stop!

> *(Beat.)*

I think you all ought to stop right now. Can't everybody put their lives on hold forever on account of one wayward dog. Though it fills my heart to see how you've all worked so hard to find him.

LANIE: We've tried our best, Charlie. We really have.

CHARLIE: I know you have, Lanie. You and Burl, tramping all over the countryside like you did.

AUDREY: I wish we had found him for you.

CHARLIE: Thank you, Audrey. I know you put up posters all over town. And I'm sorry again that I kicked you with my sister's white majorette boots. And lied to you several times—more than several. I've never played soccer in my life. And I've never even been to a ballet, nor would I want to.

AUDREY: That's okay. You was just upset about being in a new town and all.

CHARLIE: And Gus and Bertha driving every which way. And Howard. You're the best. You really are. You all go home and get some rest, now. Please.

(With downcast eyes, all exit except Charlie, Gus and Bertha. Howard turns back.)

HOWARD: Charlie. I just want you to know: You've made this little place a whole lot brighter. We're all gonna miss you.

(Howard exits.)

CHARLIE: Wishbone's not ever coming back, is he?

(Musical underscoring [10A].)

GUS: The world... It hurts sometimes. Love hurts sometimes, too.

(Gus puts an arm around Charlie's shoulder. The phone rings. Bertha goes indoors to answer it.)

BERTHA: *(From indoors:)* Hello? ... Yes...yes, alright. ... Yes, she's sure. This is what she says she wants... *Tomorrow?* ... At four. ... Alright, she'll be on that bus, then. Goodbye, Miss.

(Bertha hangs up and comes out onto the porch.)

Charlie. That was—

CHARLIE: Yes, I know.

BERTHA: She's found you another foster family, quicker than she expected. I suppose you better start packing up tonight.

(Blackout.)

SCENE 12

(Charlie, Bertha and Gus wait for the bus.)

CHARLIE: I'll be just fine waiting right here, Bertha and Gus. You can go on home now.

GUS: Oh no, Butterbean, not on your life. Gonna stay right here 'til the bus arrives.

BERTHA: Gus...I can't.

GUS: Alright, Bertha.

BERTHA: I'll just say goodbye now, Charlie, if that's okay with you. *(Close to tears:)* I...guess I didn't realize that girls grew out of Cinderella. Did you know that, Gus?

GUS: No, I didn't.

BERTHA: If I had known that...and a few other things, maybe we could have made your life here a little happier. Made our place a little more welcoming.

CHARLIE: It was nothing like that. I know you did everything you could. But I was just too far from Raleigh out here. Homesick.

BERTHA: Well, I can't be spending my whole day gabbing away by the side of the road. Here's a sandwich and some cookies for your trip. Have a safe journey, and say hello to Jackie for me—and to your mama for me, if you see her.

(Bertha exits in a hurry. Beat.)

GUS: Gonna miss you, Butterbean.

(Lights crossfade. Lights up on the representation of a bus interior.)

(Charlie sits, appearing forlorn, a suitcase at her side. The low rumbling of a bus. She imagines the voices of a number of people.)

LANIE: *(Off:)* We've tried our best, Charlie. We really did.

HOWARD: *(Off:)* There's only one person in the world who can tell you what you want. And that's you.

BERTHA: *(Off:)* We haven't had any practice being parents, Charlie. But I hope you'll be patient with us while we learn.

HOWARD: *(Off:)* My wish...was something different. It was that we could always be friends.

GUS: The world hurts sometimes. Love hurts, too.

(Musical underscoring [10B]. Jackie then appears, as if walking from the back of the bus, as vivid as in real life. Charlie looks up at her in amazement.)

JACKIE: You got Gus and Bertha loving you and treating you like a princess. You got all those Odoms thanking the good Lord for you. And that Howard is the nicest friend you could ever want. You got these beautiful mountains and a garden and a porch to sit on that's like sitting on the side of heaven. You've got family here.

(Jackie exits. Charlie looks around, taking in the mountains around her.)

CHARLIE: It was all right here. Family. *My* family. I just needed to open my eyes.

(Beat.)

Hold on! Stop!

BUS DRIVER: What is it, miss?

CHARLIE: Let me off here. Please!

BUS DRIVER: I can't do that, miss. Let me pull over and we'll talk this out—

CHARLIE: But you have to let me off! My ticket says Raleigh, but I've changed my mind. I'm going back to Colby. Back home. It's where I want to be from now on.

BUS DRIVER: Well, I can't just drop you off on the side of the road.

CHARLIE: We've only gone a couple of miles. I can walk back there. Easy! Or catch the local bus.

(Beat.)

BUS DRIVER: I'll turn around and take you back there. I don't think any of the passengers will mind too much.

(Blackout. Scene change music [10C].)

SCENE 13

(Musical underscoring continues. Bertha and Gus are seated on the porch swing or bench. Charlie sits on the steps of the porch.)

BERTHA: And then, one time we ran out of gas in the middle of nowhere with three cats in the car. Remember that, Gus?

GUS: Yep.

BERTHA: When we were a little younger, we would have loved to have a child, Gus and I. Isn't that right, Gus?

GUS: Yep.

BERTHA: But it just never worked out. *(With a contented sigh:)* 'Til now. I never in my wildest dreams would've thought we'd have a family like this, would you, Gus?

GUS: *(Wiping a tear from his eye:)* Nope. Never did.

(Charlie gets up from the steps and sits between them. Beat.)

BERTHA: *(Putting her arm around Charlie:)* You've been a blessing in this house, Charlie Reese, from the very first moment you arrived. A blessing.

GUS: You surely have been, Butterbean. You surely are.

BERTHA: And guess what I'm doing first thing tomorrow?

CHARLIE: What's that?

BERTHA: I'm getting every single one of those dang canning jars out of your room. Don't know where we're going to put them, but we'll figure it out, isn't that right, Gus?

GUS: It's about time, Bertha. And we'll figure it out.

BERTHA: Maybe in the cupboard next to the sink, if I could get you to move some of your tools out of there.

GUS: Well, I suppose I could do that. If you can move some of your sewing supplies out from under the bed —

(Wishbone appears, pausing at the edge of the stage.)

CHARLIE: Wishbone! *(Running to him:)* You're back! *(Hugging him:)* Oh, Wishbone! Where've you been, fella? It doesn't matter, does it? You're back! You're back to stay — oh! Oh my!

GUS: What is it, Butterbean?

CHARLIE: He's got a hurt paw.

GUS: Got into a couple of thorns, it looks like. We can fix him right up.

CHARLIE: Oh, Wishbone, you were chasing that old mountain lion away from here, weren't you? Chased it all the way across the state to the Atlantic Ocean, more than likely, just to protect this little family. No wonder it took you so long to find your way back home!

BERTHA: I've got just the salve in the medicine cabinet to put on that paw of his. And you know what, Wishbone? I might just have some meatloaf left over from last night's supper!

(Wishbone barks. Charlie grabs her diary, moves downstage and addresses the audience directly. Wishbone joins her. As Charlie speaks, Howard, Burl and Lanie enter with musical instruments.)

CHARLIE: Dear Diary: So I guess I'm here to stay, although I know that Jackie and I will visit each other whenever we get the chance. After all, she's got a home here, too.

(Charlie puts down her diary and may twirl once out of sheer joy. Music begins [11].)

But oh, how I wish she had been here on the mountain that night. For on the evening of the very day that I got off the bus on the outskirts of town and Wishbone reappeared, the Odom kids came by and brought their guitars and fiddle to celebrate the news that I was back.

(Exuberant dancing and clapping accompany the song.)

11. Going Home

LANIE: WELL, LAST NIGHT I DREAMED I WAS BENAIAH
AND FOUND MYSELF IN A GNARLY SPOT.
ICY WALLS ON EVERY SIDE,
AND WITH NO DANG PLACE TO HIDE,
I SAID, LION, SHOW ME WHAT YOU GOT.
'CAUSE I'M GOING HOME. I'M ON MY WAY.
I WON'T LET NO LITTLE CAT STAND IN MY WAY.
WELL, FEARS AND DOUBTS, YOU'VE HAD YOUR SAY
BUT I'LL BE GOING HOME TODAY

HOWARD: WELL, LAST NIGHT I DREAMED I WERE A PILGRIM
HOMEWARD BOUND IN DAYS OF YORE

THEN A MOUNTAIN APPEARED RIGHT IN FRONT OF ME
WHERE NONE WAS THERE BEFORE
BUT I'M GOING HOME. I'M ON MY WAY.
I WON'T LET NO LITTLE ROCK STAND IN MY WAY.
WELL, FEARS AND DOUBTS, YOU'VE HAD YOUR SAY
BUT I'LL BE GOING HOME TODAY

CHARLIE: WELL, LAST NIGHT I DREAMED I WAS A
BLUEBIRD.
I WAS FLYING THROUGH AN AWFUL GALE.
BUT WHEN I SAW A DISTANT BEACON,
THEN MY HEART BECAME A SAIL.
WELL, IT SHINED RIGHT THROUGH THOSE STORM
CLOUDS
FOR ALL THE WORLD TO SEE.
IT WAS SHINING DOWN WITH LOVE
FROM THE HEAVENS HIGH ABOVE.
IT WAS SHINING JUST FOR ME.
'CAUSE I'M GOING HOME. I'M ON MY WAY.
I WON'T LET NO LITTLE STORM STAND IN MY WAY
WELL, FEARS AND DOUBTS, YOU'VE HAD YOUR SAY
BUT I'LL BE GOING HOME TODAY

ENSEMBLE: I'M GOING HOME. I'M ON MY WAY.
I WON'T LET NO LITTLE STORM STAND IN MY WAY.
WELL, FEARS AND DOUBTS, YOU'VE HAD YOUR SAY
BUT I'LL BE GOING HOME TODAY!

BERTHA: Star! First star! Everybody make a wish, now!

*(Music pauses at the fermata. All look up, then Charlie turns to
speak directly to the audience.)*

CHARLIE: Now, you might think that I gave up wishing, on
account of what I said to Howard. But Howard was actually
right, as he almost always is. I can't give up wishing for very

long. Wishing is part of who I am. And so we sang and carried on. And the stars all came out—millions of stars.

(Music resumes. As Charlie continues to speak, Audrey enters, joining the others. Soon all are arrayed across the stage, gazing up at the starry sky which has come into view.)

And Gus, who knows all about the stars and constellations, spent the longest time giving us a tour of all the different corners of the starry sky. Even Audrey came by, and pretty soon everybody was just standing there, studying the sky.

(The constellation Pegasus comes into view.)

And finally the constellation Pegasus became visible in the southeastern sky, and I happened to know that Pegasus, the winged horse, was an especially fortunate sight in the world of wishing, so I told everyone that if they had any special wishes, this would be the time to wish them. But even with all of those folks around me—this family of mine—wishing from the deepest part of their hearts, when I looked up at Pegasus soaring over the mountains, instead of wishing, I just closed my eyes and breathed in the piney air, the wet-dog Wishbone smell and the fine aroma of huckleberry pie cooling off in the kitchen. Here I was at last, in my home beneath the stars, surrounded by the family I had been wishing for all along. And for the first time that I can remember, I didn't wish for anything at all. Because my wish had finally come true.

(Music swells. Blackout.)

(Curtain Call [11A].)

(Bluegrass.)

(End of play.)

The Author Speaks

What inspired you to write this play?

When I read Barbara O'Connor's novel *Wish*, I was immediately taken by the narrative voice of its young protagonist, Charlie—observant, opinionated, scrappy and trying to find the best version of herself while buffeted by a volatile mix of anger, longing and optimism. I thought her story would lend itself wonderfully to the stage. There is, too, a compelling specificity to the Blue Ridge Mountains setting of the book, which suggested to me a bluegrass-heavy score, the idea of which I found fun and exciting.

Was the structure or some other element of the play influenced by any other work?

Like so many of our best stories, this one is, in essence, a journey. For Charlie, it's a journey to an unfamiliar and very foreign part of her state of North Carolina, but also an inner journey of self-awareness, discovery and growth, all of which occur during her single-minded quest to find "home." As I was writing this musical, I occasionally thought of Homer's *The Odyssey* as well as *The Wizard of Oz* as examples of similar journeys, although on a more epic scale.

Have you dealt with the same theme(s) in other works that you have written?

This is really a story about finding family in the most unlikely of places, and I don't believe I've written about that before. But underpinning the story are themes that come up all the time in my writing: navigating adversity, staying true to your own heart and—perhaps most importantly of all—recognizing love when you find it.

What writers have had the most profound effect on your style?

Being a songwriter inevitably informs my dialogue to some

degree. I pay a lot of attention to how the words look on the page and how they might sound. I value economy of expression, dangerous choices and emotional resonance. I most admire Stephen Sondheim for all of these qualities. I also love the writing of Arthur Miller for some of the same reasons.

What were the biggest challenges involved in the writing of this play? For example, was there a particular moment that was difficult to write, and if so, why?

An adaptation of an existing work is, in itself, a challenge. Barbara's book is 227 pages long, so obviously there is a lot of storytelling in the book that got left out of the musical. In adapting the novel, my goals were to establish an authentic sense of place — that of Charlie's singular world — and to create a compelling dramatic arc in a little over an hour of stage time. I did spend an inordinate amount of time on the opening scene and song. Opening numbers are notoriously difficult, and this one had a great deal of lifting to do: backstory and exposition, the beginning of a journey and establishing both the tone of the overall piece as well as the protagonist's voice. I'm pretty happy with the result.

What is your playwriting "origin story"?

Playwriting is really all about telling stories. When I think about it, my inspiration for becoming a storyteller probably came from my dad, who, as far as I recall, didn't read to my brothers and me but told great, nearly cinematic, made-up stories using a recurrent cast of comically tragic and vaudevillian characters. I also listened to an excessive number of Broadway musicals when I was growing up; they served as another model of singular American storytelling for me.

How did you research the subject? Are any characters modeled after real life or historical figures?

Barbara's novel was my primary source material. I also

listened to a great deal of bluegrass and country music to immerse myself in those musical vernaculars and discovered some amazing musical artists along the way. I got so carried away, in fact, that I took up the pedal steel guitar as I was writing this musical, much to the consternation of my wife.

What is your writing process?

It varies from project to project, but I usually don't write linearly, preferring instead to write out key songs and beats first. I'll then try to map out a way to link all of these various landmarks. Having said that, I try not to get wedded too tightly to even that kind of roadmap, because once the script develops a center of gravity and momentum, the characters themselves often begin to suggest their own best lines and exercise the most surprising choices.

Shakespeare gave advice to the players in *Hamlet*; if you could give advice to your cast, what would it be?

What struck me most about the characters in this musical is their essential decency and goodness. (In fact, there is no antagonist in this story, which I found rather interesting.) If you take away the regional speech and customs and other superficial trappings, it's the goodness that remains. If I were to give any notes to a future cast, it would be to avoid caricature and instead look inward to find the authentic voices of their characters.

How was the first production different from the vision that you created in your mind?

This show's first production was a live performance at a youth theatre festival, filmed for an online audience, courtesy of the pandemic. The lack of an audience was jarring to me, and I felt a lot of empathy and respect for the cast to have put in such a mighty effort on this project without the reward of an audience in the room.

When you're not writing, what might we find you doing?
Playing pedal steel guitar while listening to recordings of Nancy Griffith, John Prine and other extraordinary singer-songwriters.

Have you ever actually been to the Blue Ridge Mountains of North Carolina?
Yes—on a car camping trip with my best friend from high school. For reasons which still remain unexplained, my friend, whom I'll call J., suddenly got terribly homesick for Cleveland and insisted on breaking camp and driving home in the middle of our second night there. Although this was many years ago, I still have fond memories of the verdant hills and the friendly people we encountered while in the area.

About the Author

Paul Lewis is a Seattle-based playwright and composer whose work includes musical adaptations of two iconic children's books—*The Runaway Bunny* and *Caps for Sale*—both of which premiered at Boston Children's Theatre; *Lost in the Hills*, a musical adapted from a novel by Zane Grey; *Jill Trent Science Sleuth* (Cayuga College); *The Crossing, A Musical* (Theater Schmeater and Jewel Box Theatre), winner of a Seattle Times Footlights Award for promising new work; the full-length play *Oblivion* (Driftwood); and *The Hours of Life, A Musical* (Theatre22). His play *The Names* has had developmental readings at Equity Library Theatre of Chicago, FUSION, Atlantic Stage and The Field (NYC). Paul's one-act plays have been staged at theatres across North America and the UK, winning Best of Festival awards at a number of these. He is a member of BMI and the Dramatists Guild of America.

About YouthPLAYS

YouthPLAYS (www.youthplays.com) is a publisher of award-winning professional dramatists and talented new discoveries, each with an original theatrical voice, and all dedicated to expanding the vocabulary of theatre for young actors and audiences. On our website, you'll find one-act and full-length plays and musicals for teen and pre-teen (and even college) actors, as well as duets and monologues for competition. Many of our authors' works have been widely produced at high schools and middle schools, youth theatres and other TYA companies, both amateur and professional, as well as at elementary schools, camps, churches and other institutions serving young audiences and/or actors worldwide. Most are intended for performance by young people, while some are intended for adult actors performing for young audiences.

YouthPLAYS was co-founded by professional playwrights Jonathan Dorf and Ed Shockley. It began merely as an additional outlet to market their own works, which included a substantial body of award-winning published and unpublished plays and musicals. Those interested in their published plays were directed to the respective publishers' websites, and unpublished plays were made available in electronic form. But when they saw the desperate need for material for young actors and audiences—coupled with their experience that numerous quality plays for young people weren't finding a home—they made the decision to represent the work of other playwrights as well. Dozens and dozens of authors are now members of the YouthPLAYS family, with scripts available both electronically and in traditional acting editions. We continue to grow as we look for exciting and challenging plays and musicals for young actors and audiences.

About ProduceaPlay.com

Let's put up a play! Great idea! But producing a play takes time, energy and knowledge. While finding the necessary time and energy is up to you, ProduceaPlay.com is a website designed to assist you with that third element: knowledge.

Created by YouthPLAYS' co-founders, Jonathan Dorf and Ed Shockley, ProduceaPlay.com serves as a resource for producers at all levels as it addresses the many facets of production. As Dorf and Shockley speak from their years of experience (as playwrights, producers, directors and more), they are joined by a group of award-winning theatre professionals and experienced teachers from the world of academic theatre, all making their expertise available for free in the hope of helping this and future generations of producers, whether it's at the school or university level, or in community or professional theatres.

The site is organized into a series of major topics, each of which has its own page that delves into the subject in detail, offering suggestions and links for further information. For example, Publicity covers everything from Publicizing Auditions to How to Use Social Media to Posters to whether it's worth hiring a publicist. Casting details Where to Find the Actors, How to Evaluate a Resume, Callbacks and even Dealing with Problem Actors. You'll find guidance on your Production Timeline, The Theater Space, Picking a Play, Budget, Contracts, Rehearsing the Play, The Program, House Management, Backstage, and many other important subjects.

The site is constantly under construction, so visit often for the latest insights on play producing, and let it help make your play production dreams a reality.

More from YouthPLAYS

The Bremen Town Black Cat Band by Paul Lewis
Dramedy with music. 45-55 minutes. 1-6+ females, 2-7+ males, 5 any (8-29+ performers possible).

What do you do when the formerly affectionate couple who raised you chases you away from the only home you've ever known? If you're Caruso, a talented accordion-playing donkey in Bavaria, you hit the road. There, Caruso joins up with three other talented animals: Dog, who plays the washboard; Cat, a vocalist and washtub bass player; and Rooster, who specializes in the kazoo. Together, they perform to great acclaim in Bremen Town, but Caruso longs for home and his parents. With the aid of his musician friends, the wayward donkey returns, but will he solve the mystery of his sudden exile? And is there any chance for a miraculous reunion with his parents?

Anne of Green Gables by Donna Hoke
Drama. 100-120 minutes. 6-14 females, 2-5 males, 1+ any gender (9-20+ performers possible).

When Matthew and Marilla Cuthbert decide to take in a foster child, they request a boy. Imagine their surprise when Anne, a girl of boundless imagination with a mouth to match, shows up on their doorstep. Still, the two of them take a chance on her in hopes they can do some good. As Anne comes of age, her curiosity and wonder may get her in trouble, but ultimately her capacity for love teaches them all what it means to create and commit to family in this inventive and timeless free adaptation of the heartwarming classic by L.M. Montgomery.

The Old New Kid by Adam J. Goldberg
Comedy. 30-40 minutes. 3-10+ females, 2-9+ males (8-30+ performers possible).

It's the half-day of school before Thanksgiving break, and current "new kid" Alan Socrates Bama just wants to get through the day. But when a new-new kid arrives, things change. Alan has three hours to find the meaning of Thanksgiving, survive elementary school politics, battle for his identity, and spell the word "cornucopia" in this *Peanuts*-flavored comedy for kids of all ages.

Caliban's Island by Diana Burbano
Dramedy. 50-60 minutes. 2 females, 2 males, 1 any gender.

Characters from Shakespeare's **Twelfth Night** and **The Tempest** intertwine as a pair of twins are shipwrecked on an island, encountering a half-human "monster," fairies and a young girl with magical powers who has been there since babyhood. Mortals will struggle with the magical; loyalty will wrestle with love, and wishes, dreams, and wisdom will collide, leaving no one unchanged.

The Prince and the Pauper by Andrew Beattie
Historical Dramedy. 120 minutes. 5+ females, 9+ males (14-80+ performers possible).

In Tudor England, two boys grow up in very different worlds: One is the son of Henry VIII and heir to the throne, the other scrapes by in the slums of London. When a chance encounter offers them an opportunity to escape their fates for the day and see how the "other half lives," they eagerly swap clothes and change places in each other's lives. But what begins as a lark turns into a series of eye-opening and harrowing adventures, and if the boys can't manage to set things right in time, a pauper from Offal Court could end up the next king of England in this play based on the Mark Twain classic.

Rumpelstiltskin, The Game of the Name by
Catherine Hurd (book & lyrics) & Vatrena King (music)
Musical. 80-90 minutes. 5 females, 6 males, 2+ any gender
(13-30+ performers possible).

What do you do when your father claims you can spin straw
into gold? If you're Jane, daughter of the town miller, you end
up imprisoned in the castle tower by the King and told to prove
it. Jane has three days and nights: If she can turn straw into
gold, she gets to marry the Prince, but if she fails, she and her
father will be locked up forever. Just as all seems lost, a
magical man appears from the shadows, offering salvation...at
a terrible price. Will Jane find a way to free herself from this
devil's bargain and claim her happily ever after in this musical
adaptation of the fairy tale classic?

Hula Heart by Velina Hasu Houston
Dramedy. 50-60 minutes. 5 females, 2 males.

A young boy moves from Hawaii to suburban California only to
find that his love for the sacred rites of hula doesn't transfer
quite as easily. As Kalā struggles to find his way in this new
life, he wonders where his old culture fits in—and how he can
make both the old and the new fit together. Maybe the answer
lies in discovering what's most important in life.

Cuentos de Josefina by Gregory Ramos
Folktale with music. 100-110 minutes. 6+ females, 4+ males
(10-50+ performers possible).

A heartfelt memory tale that follows the story of young
Josefina and her brother Ignacio's journey from Mexico to the
United States after the Mexican revolution. The play explores
what it means to leave one land in search of another, and the
value in maintaining ties to our past. Based on true Mexican
family tales, ***Cuentos de Josefina (Josephine's Tales)***
weaves together a series of stories that can be told with
various theatrical devices, including story theatre, movement,
music, shadow and puppetry.

Made in the USA
Columbia, SC
30 June 2024